Text copyright © Pat Thomas 2006
Illustrations copyright © Lesley Harker 2006
First published in 2006 by Hodder Children's Books

Editor: Kirsty Hamilton
Concept design: Kate Buxton
Series design: Jean Scott Moncrieff

British Library Cataloguing in Publication Data
Thomas, Pat, 1959-
Do I have to go to hospital? : a first look at going to hospital
1.Hospitals - Pictorial works - Juvenile literature
I. Title
362.1'1

ISBN 0340 894512

Printed in China

Hodder Children's Books
A division of Hodder Headline Limited
338, Euston Road,
London NW1 3BH

Do I Have to Go to Hospital?

A FIRST LOOK AT GOING TO HOSPITAL

PAT THOMAS
ILLUSTRATED BY LESLEY HARKER

Hodder
Children's
Books

a division of Hodder Headline Limited

It's not much fun
being sick.

When you are sick you don't feel much like playing or talking or eating, so there's not very much to do.

Most of the time when you are hurt or ill you
can get better at home. Your parents know a
lot about how to take care of you.

They know how to bandage your knee, take your temperature, tuck you up nice and warm in bed and give you lots of cuddles to help you feel better.

What about you?

What do your parents do to help you feel better when you are sick?

But sometimes when you are very sick its best to
have a doctor or a nurse help look after you.

This may mean a
visit to the doctor's
office or even to
the hospital.

Sometimes your parents and your doctors plan for
you to go to hospital for special treatment.

But some visits to the hospital are not planned.

Some people only need to stay in hospital for a few hours, but sometimes you need to stay longer.

What about you?

Can you think of some reasons why people go to hospital? Have you ever been to a hospital?

13

Going into hospital can be scary. Hospitals are big, busy places. You may hear new noises and smell new smells.

There may be lots of people you don't know and who don't know you.

That's why you will be given a special bracelet with your name on it. The doctors and nurses wear badges with their names too.

The doctors and nurses
in hospitals have gone
to special schools to
learn lots of ways of
making you feel better.

Your parents trust them and you can too.

What about you?

How do you feel about going to hospital? Is there anything that worries you? Any questions you would like to ask?

17

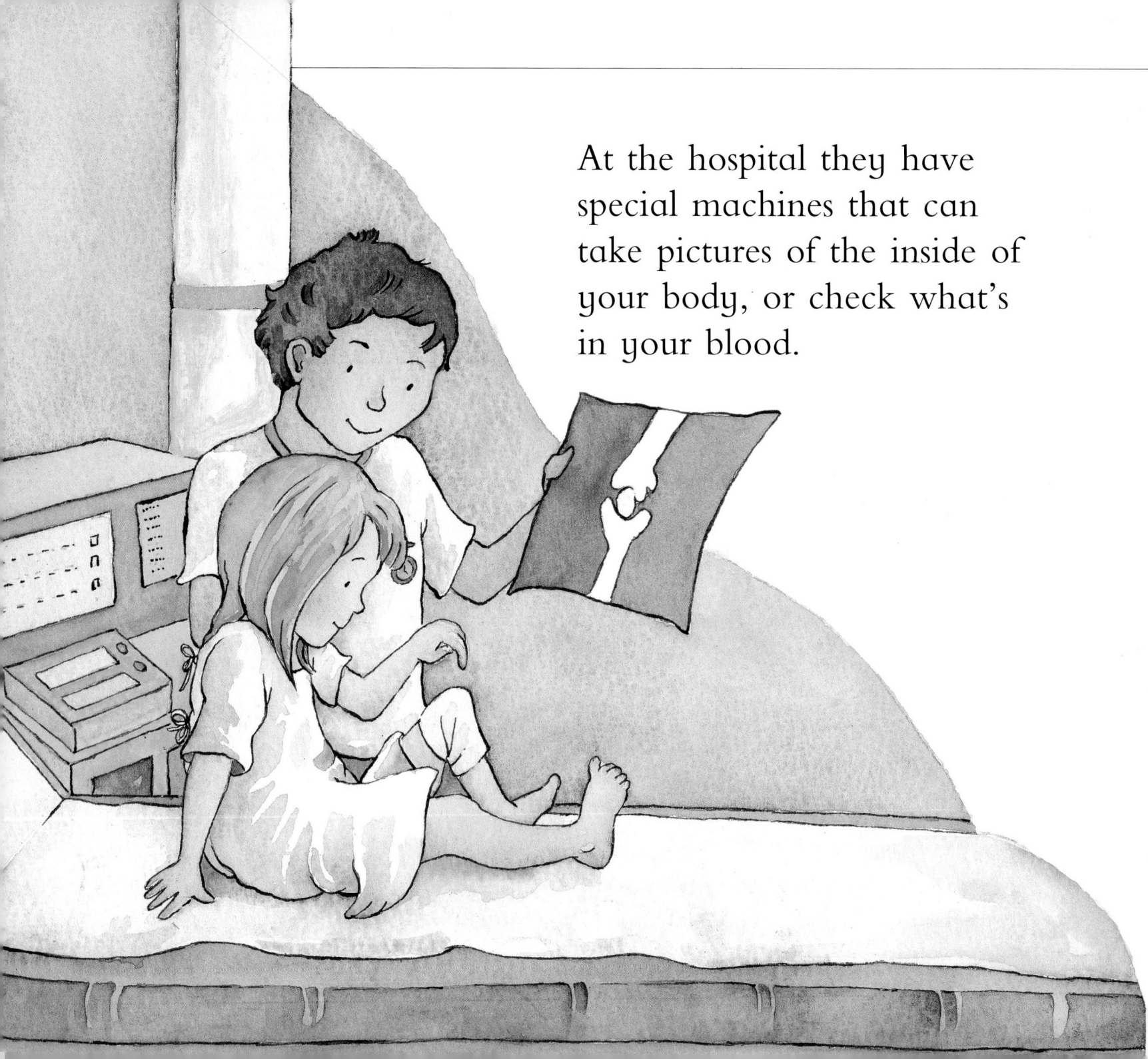

At the hospital they have special machines that can take pictures of the inside of your body, or check what's in your blood.

They have tools for listening to your heartbeat and mending broken bones.

They also have special medicines to help you get better.

There may be other children there and you may share a room with one or more of them.

This means you will have someone to talk to and keep you company.

You can still do things like play games and watch
television while you are in hospital.

And there will be a telephone so you can talk to your friends and family if you need to.

Your parents will be able to stay at the hospital and you may also have visitors.

They can bring
you toys and books
and tell you all
about what is
happening at home.

Nobody likes going to hospital.
But sometimes you really do
have to.

And because of all the special care you are getting it won't be long before you are feeling better and are happy to be home.

HOW TO USE THIS BOOK

Hospitals can be undermining for parents and frightening for children. Whatever treatment your child needs you can help make the experience more positive by making sure that your child is allowed to express feelings and ask questions. A child who is adequately prepared for what will happen in hospital will find the adjustment much easier than one who is not. You know your child best and already have the skills to help. However here are some things to consider:

This book focuses mostly on the emotional experience of hospital rather than specific procedures. Whatever procedures your child needs, make sure you find a way to explain them in language that is simple and reassuring but which is, at the same time, not misleading. For instance, don't say something won't hurt when it will, don't promise a quick release from hospital if your child needs an extended stay. If you don't know the answer to a specific question it is OK to say so. But also make a promise that you will find out more from the doctor.

Try to stay calm. Your child can pick up on your level of fear and be frightened by this. You can ease your own fears by asking questions beforehand about what will happen. It can help to make a list of questions to ask before any meeting with a doctor and if you don't understand the answer ask the doctor to explain it to you again in a way you can understand.

Allow your children to feel whatever they are feeling about going to hospital without judgement. Occasionally parents want their children to reassure them by 'being good' about going into hospital. As an adult it is your job to do the reassuring. Instead of insisting on a positive attitude, find out what is behind the fear. It could be a lack of understanding of the condition, unanswered questions about procedures especially if they involve surgery, scary stories other children have told them, a previous negative experience in hospital or even fear of dying. You'll never know unless you gently help your children to talk about it.

Play doctor with your children. Bandage a teddy bear's or doll's arm, put its foot in a pretend cast or pretend to take a blood sample. All of these things will help familiarise your child with the kinds of procedures they may be exposed to in hospital.

Schools can help familiarise children with the concept of hospitals by arranging visits from nurses and doctors in the local community who can talk to them about what hospitals are and what happens there. There is ample evidence that such visits can help children cope better should they eventually have to go to hospital.

BOOKS TO READ

'I Don't Want to go to Hospital'
Tony Ross
(Anderson Press 2000)

'Say Aah!'
Jen Green and Mike Gordon
(Hodder Wayland 2000)

'Separations – Hospital'
Janine Amos
(Cherrytree Press 1998)

'Topsy and Tim go to Hospital'
Jean and Gareth Adamson
(Ladybird 1998)

'Going to the Doctor'
Anne Civardi
(Usborne First Experiences 2000)

'Going to the Hospital'
Anne Civardi and Stephen Cartwright
(Usborne First Experiences 1992)

RESOURCES FOR ADULTS

Action For Sick Children
c/o National Children's Bureau
8 Wakley Street
London EC1V 7QE
020 7843 6444
www.actionforsickchildren.org

The UK's leading children's healthcare charity,
set up to ensure that sick children's needs are
taken into account and that the whole child is
treated, not just their injury or illness, whether
at home, in hospital or in the community.
Publications available.

Children First for Health
P.O. Box 49717
London
WC1N 3WY
0845 122 86 36 (Wellchild helpline)
www.childrenfirst.nhs.uk

NHS based service to provide children and
families with quality health information: links
to support groups, information about what to
expect in hospital and information about
individual hospitals, a safe forum for sharing
experiences and more.